REFLECTIONS
FOR
LENT, HOLY WEEK
AND
EASTER

Wednesday 18 February –
Saturday 11 April 2026

ISABELLE HAMLEY
BEN QUASH
CARLTON TURNER

with Holy Week and Easter Week reflections
by
RACHEL TREWEEK

Church House Publishing
Church House
27 Great Smith Street
London SW1P 3AZ

ISBN 978 1 78140 522 2

Published 2025 by Church House Publishing
Copyright © The Archbishops' Council 2025

The opinions expressed in this book are those of the authors and do not necessarily reflect the official policy of the General Synod or The Archbishops' Council of the Church of England.

Series editor: Catherine Williams
Liturgical editor: Peter Moger
Designed and typeset by Hugh Hillyard-Parker
Printed and bound by CPI Group (UK) Ltd, Croydon, CR0 4YY

EU GPSR Authorised Representative
LOGOS EUROPE, 9 rue Nicolas Poussin,
17000, LA ROCHELLE, France
E-mail: Contact@logoseurope.eu

What do you think of *Reflections for Lent*?

We'd love to hear from you – simply email us at

publishing@churchofengland.org

or write to us at

Church House Publishing, Church House,
27 Great Smith Street, London SW1P 3AZ.

Visit **www.dailyprayer.org.uk** for more information on the *Reflections* series, ordering and subscriptions.

Contents

About the authors

Isabelle Hamley is a theologian, speaker and broadcaster. She is currently principal of Ridley Hall Cambridge, after holding posts as parish priest, university chaplain, chaplain to the Archbishop of Canterbury and theological adviser to the House of Bishops. She has a particular interest in the Old Testament and questions of justice, identity and mental health.

Mark Oakley is Dean of Southwark. Prior to this he was Dean and Fellow of St John's College, Cambridge. He is also Honorary Canon Theologian of Wakefield Cathedral in the Diocese of Leeds. He is the author of *The Collage of God* (2001), *The Splash of Words: Believing in Poetry* (2016) and *My Sour Sweet Days: George Herbert and the Journey of the Soul* (2019) as well as numerous articles and reviews, usually in the areas of faith, poetry, human rights and literature. He is a Fellow of King's College London, where he is also a Visiting Lecturer.

Ben Quash is Professor of Christianity and the Arts at King's College London, where he directs the Centre for Arts & the Sacred at King's, and the Visual Commentary on Scripture (thevcs.org). He is Canon Theologian of Bradford and Coventry Cathedrals, and Honorary Assistant Priest in the Diocese of Ely.

Rachel Treweek was consecrated as the 41st Bishop of Gloucester in 2015 and made history by becoming the first female diocesan bishop and the first female bishop in the House of Lords. Her role in the House of Lords includes being the Anglican Bishop for HM Prisons in England and Wales.

Carlton Turner is tutor in Contextual Theology and Mission Studies at the Queen's Foundation, Birmingham. As a Caribbean Contextual and Practical Theologian, he explores the intersections of Christian theology and decoloniality, particularly within the British imperial history and context

About *Reflections for Lent, Holy Week and Easter*

Based on the *Common Worship Lectionary* readings for Morning Prayer, these daily reflections are designed to refresh and inspire times of personal prayer. The aim is to provide rich, contemporary and engaging insights into Scripture.

Each page lists the lectionary readings for the day, with the main psalms for that day highlighted in **bold**. The collect of the day – either the *Common Worship* collect or the shorter additional collect – is also included.

For those using this book in conjunction with a service of Morning Prayer, the following conventions apply: a psalm printed in parentheses is omitted if it has been used as the opening canticle at that office; a psalm marked with an asterisk may be shortened if desired.

A short reflection is provided on either the Old or New Testament reading. Popular writers, experienced ministers, biblical scholars and theologians contribute to this series, all bringing their own emphases, enthusiasms and approaches to biblical interpretation.

Regular users of Morning Prayer and *Time to Pray* (from *Common Worship: Daily Prayer*) and anyone who follows the Lectionary for their regular Bible reading will benefit from the rich variety of traditions represented in these stimulating and accessible pieces.

The book also includes both a simple form of Common Worship: Morning Prayer (see pages 52–53) and a short form of Night Prayer, also known as Compline (see pages 56–59), particularly for the benefit of those readers who are new to the habit of the Daily Office or for any reader while travelling.

Lent – jousting within the self

It has been said that the heart of the human problem is the problem of the human heart. Lent is time set aside each year to take this thought seriously.

A few years ago, there was a story in the papers about a painting by Pieter Bruegel the Elder. It is currently on display in Vienna's marvellous Kunsthistorisches Museum, but Krakow's National Museum claims it is theirs and that it was stolen by the wife of the city's Nazi governor in 1939 during the occupation of Poland.

The painting is called 'The Fight Between Carnival and Lent' and it was painted in 1559. It is a beautifully typical Bruegel painting. It is a large, crowded canvas with nearly 200 men, women and children depicted on it. We find ourselves looking down on a town square during a riotous festival. The painting can be looked at in two halves. On the right, we see a church with people leaving after prayer. We see them giving alms to the poor, feeding the hungry, helping those with disability, calling attention to their need and tending to the dying. On the left, we see an inn. Congregated around it are beer drinkers, gamblers, various saucy types. The vulnerable nearby are not noticed, including a solitary procession of lepers. Instead, a man vomits out of a window and another bangs his head against a wall.

In the foreground, we see two figures being pulled towards each other on floats. One is Lady Lent, gaunt and unshowy, dressed as a nun, with followers eating pretzels and fish as well as drawing fresh water from a large well. The other is Carnival, a fat figure, armed with a meat spit and a pork pie helmet. He's followed by masked carousers. A man in yellow – the symbolic colour of deceit – pushes his float, though he looks rather weighed down by cups and a bag of belongings. In the background, we see, on the left, some stark, leafless trees, but on the right side, buds are awakening on the branches and, as if to see them better, a woman is busily cleaning her windows.

It is an allegorical delight, and we might do worse than take a close look at it sometime this Lent. It's tempting to classify each human there as either good or bad, secular or faithful, kind or indifferent. We love to place people into convenient cutlery trays, dividing us all up as is most useful for us. What I love about this painting, however, is that it reminds me that we are all similarly made with two halves.

For so many of us, there is a constant fight going on within between the times we are negligent and the times we are careful; days in which we get through with a self that enjoys its own attention, being centre-stage, and days when our self just feels somehow more itself when not being selfish. I have an impulse to pray; I have an impulse to avoid or forget it. There are parts of me grotesquely masked, and there are parts of me trying to clean my windows on a ladder, as it were, wanting to increase transparency and attention to the world, to me and to my relationships.

Lent begins with a small dusty cross being made on my head, the hard case that protects the organ that makes decisions. The season starts by asking me to imagine how life might be if the imprint of Christ's courageous compassion might make itself felt and acted on, rather than just passionately talked about. Lent knows what we are like. It has seen the painting. It has read a bit of Freud, some history books, political manifestos and memoirs of hurt and achievement. It winces at our cyclical, self-destructive repetitions. It believes in us, though, knowing that, with God and each other, if we reach outside of our own hardened little worlds, we set the scene to be helped and, maybe, even changed. That would be good – for me and those who live with me.

In the Gospels, the 40 days Jesus spent in the beguiling wilderness immediately followed his baptism. Coming up out of the water, he had heard the unmistakable voice that matters, telling him he was cherished, wanted and ready. He then goes into the heat spending time with himself, hearing other voices that want him to live down to them; but he knows that his vocation can only be lived when he learns to live up to the one voice he heard that day in the river, not down to the ones that want him to live some conventionally indifferent and submerged existence as a consumer of the world and not as a citizen of the kingdom. We follow him. Where he goes, so do we. A wilderness Lent is needed more than ever to do some heart-repair and start becoming Christians again.

I don't know who owns the Bruegel painting. What I do know is that its themes belong to all of us; our inner landscape matches his rowdy town square. As long as the fight continues, the soul will be alive.

Mark Oakley

Building daily prayer into daily life

In our morning routines there are many tasks we do without giving much thought to them, and others that we do with careful attention. Daily prayer and Bible reading is a strange mixture of these. These are disciplines (and gifts) that we as Christians should have in our daily pattern, but they are not tasks to be ticked off. Rather they are a key component of our developing relationship with God. In them is *life* – for the fruits of this time are to be lived out by us – and to be most fruitful, the task requires both purpose and letting go.

In saying a daily office of prayer, we make a deliberate decision to spend time with God – the God who is always with us. In prayer and attentive reading of the Scriptures, there is both a conscious entering into God's presence and a 'letting go' of all we strive to control: both are our acknowledgement that it is God who is God.

> ... *come before his presence with a song...*
>
> *Know that the Lord is God;*
> *it is he that has made us and we are his;*
> *we are his people and the sheep of his pasture.*
>
> *Enter his gates with thanksgiving...*
>
> *(Psalm 100, a traditional Canticle at Morning Prayer)*

If we want a relationship with someone to deepen and grow, we need to spend time with that person. It can be no surprise that the same is true between us and God.

In our daily routines, I suspect that most of us intentionally look in the mirror; occasionally we might see beyond the surface of our external reflection and catch a glimpse of who we truly are. For me, a regular pattern of daily prayer and Bible reading is like a hard look in a clean mirror: it gives a clear reflection of myself, my life and the world in which I live. But it is more than that, for in it I can also see the reflection of God who is most clearly revealed in Jesus Christ and present with us now in the Holy Spirit.

This commitment to daily prayer is about our relationship with the God who is love. St Paul, in his great passage about love, speaks of now seeing 'in a mirror, dimly' but one day seeing face to face: 'Now I know only in part; then I will know fully, even as I have been fully known' (1 Corinthians 13.12). Our daily prayer is part of that seeing in a mirror dimly, and it is also part of our deep yearning for an ever-clearer vision of our God. As we read Scripture, the past and the future converge in the present moment. We hear words from long ago – some of which can appear strange and confusing – and yet, the Holy Spirit is living and active in the present. In this place of relationship and revelation, we open ourselves to the possibility of being changed, of being reshaped in a way that is good for us and all creation.

It is important that the words of prayer and scripture should penetrate deep within rather than be a mere veneer. A quiet location is therefore a helpful starting point. For some, domestic circumstances or daily schedule make that difficult, but it is never impossible to become more fully present to God. The depths of our being can still be accessed no matter the world's clamour and activity. An awareness of this is all part of our journey from a false sense of control to a place of letting go, to a place where there is an opportunity for transformation.

Sometimes in our attention to Scripture there will be connection with places of joy or pain; we might be encouraged or provoked or both. As we look and see and encounter God more deeply, there will be thanksgiving and repentance; the cries of our heart will surface as we acknowledge our needs and desires for ourselves and the world. The liturgy of Morning Prayer gives this voice and space.

I find it helpful to begin Morning Prayer by lighting a candle. This marks my sense of purpose and my acknowledgement of Christ's presence with me. It is also a silent prayer for illumination as I prepare to be attentive to what I see in the mirror, both of myself and of God. Amid the revelation of Scripture and the cries of my heart, the constancy of the tiny flame bears witness to the hope and light of Christ in all that is and will be.

When the candle is extinguished, I try to be still as I watch the smoke disappear. For me, it is symbolic of my prayers merging with the day. I know that my prayer and the reading of Scripture are not the smoke and mirrors of delusion. Rather, they are about encounter and discovery as I seek to venture into the day to love and serve the Lord as a disciple of Jesus Christ.

+ Rachel Treweek

Wednesday 18 February
Ash Wednesday

Psalm **38**
Daniel 9.3-6, 17-19
1 Timothy 6.6-19

Daniel 9.3-6, 17-19
'... we have sinned and done wrong' (v.5)

It is easy to make a general confession: to accept that we are far from perfect, get things wrong, and ask for mercy. It is considerably harder to make a specific confession – to name those things that need to be named and take responsibility for our part, whether through weakness, brokenness or our deliberate fault. Confession is not easy, but it has been made easier by being individualized and internalized. We confess our own sins 'in our hearts before God'. And this is important.

But what does it mean to confess together, as a group, as people who belong to a church, a community, a nation, an entire world? Daniel, in this passage, is not making a personal, private, confession. He is confessing with the rest of a nation, for their corporate responsibility before God. He is not confessing the sins of others – he stands with the nation.

Underlying Daniel's prayer is the sense that all of us are part of systems, communities and networks that we cannot abstract ourselves from. We are part of their brokenness and contribute to the brokenness of the world. Daniel is bringing the whole human person before God in confession here: as individuals and as people-in-relation, as corporate persons. On Ash Wednesday, how do we bring the whole of who we are – the worlds and systems we represent before God – and name their reality and our complicity?

COLLECT

| Almighty and everlasting God,
| you hate nothing that you have made
| and forgive the sins of all those who are penitent:
| create and make in us new and contrite hearts
| that we, worthily lamenting our sins
| and acknowledging our wretchedness,
| may receive from you, the God of all mercy,
| perfect remission and forgiveness;
| through Jesus Christ our Lord.

| *Reflection by* **Isabelle Hamley**

Psalm **77** *or* 56, **57** (63*)
Genesis 39
Galatians 2.11-end

Thursday 19 February

Genesis 39

'The Lord was with Joseph' (vv.2, 21)

How do we recognize the presence of God at work around us? Stories of faith and God's action often celebrate a change in circumstances, normally for the better: an answer to prayer, unexpected joy, blessing of a sort. Of course, the presence of God cannot be confined to the good parts of life; otherwise, God turns into a cosmic Santa, which leaves those in precarious places without answers. What does it mean for God to be with us in good and bad times?

We do not hear Joseph's voice in the story. Whoever is telling the story, much later, can see God at work. God was there when Joseph was a slave, albeit a prosperous and successful slave. And God was there when Joseph was a disgraced slave, languishing in prison, because he was, once again, vulnerable before those more powerful than him.

Yet 'the Lord was with Joseph'. It would be easy to think the Lord was with him because he got him out – eventually. But that is not what the story says. The Lord was with him even when no rescue was in sight. God was in the house of slavery, in the prison, and 'showed him steadfast love'. And this love seemed most present in enabling Joseph to serve those who had power over him: Potiphar and the jailer. God's presence enabled Joseph to gain favour, not out of arbitrary, unfair preference, but out of service and diligence.

Holy God,
our lives are laid open before you:
rescue us from the chaos of sin
and through the death of your Son
bring us healing and make us whole
in Jesus Christ our Lord.

COLLECT

Reflection by **Isabelle Hamley**

7

Friday 20 February

Psalms **3**, 7 *or* **5 I**, 54
Genesis 40
Galatians 3.1-14

Genesis 40

'... remember me when it is well with you' (v.14)

Pain can build walls higher than any prison. Suffering can make someone feel isolated, misunderstood and forgotten. It can also cause others to withdraw, tired, unsure or scared. Suffering at the hand of the powerful isolates even further, because to draw near those who suffer means risking your own welfare.

Joseph is languishing in prison, no matter how much he helps the jailer. His charmed life as a boy must seem very far away. The loved son is reduced to pleading with fellow prisoners that they may return a favour. His plea, 'Remember me' speaks of his desperation and his need for human connection that goes beyond being valued for his usefulness.

'Remember me' will be the recurrent cry of the Hebrews oppressed in Exodus; it is a recurrent cry from the Psalmists facing hardship. Suffering makes you feel forsaken. The cupbearer fails the challenge. Offered grace, he fails to remember. He does not extend fellowship in suffering and simply looks to his own ends.

It is easy to forget others, particularly in the face of good fortune; yet we are called to weep with those who weep. As individuals, as churches, and as nations we are all called to remember – remember those parts of the world that do not make it to the news; remember those we choose to look away from in our streets and communities; remember those who have touched our lives, and then vanished.

COLLECT

Almighty and everlasting God,
you hate nothing that you have made
and forgive the sins of all those who are penitent:
create and make in us new and contrite hearts
that we, worthily lamenting our sins
and acknowledging our wretchedness,
may receive from you, the God of all mercy,
perfect remission and forgiveness;
through Jesus Christ our Lord.

Reflection by **Isabelle Hamley**

Saturday 21 February

Genesis 41.1-24

'It is not I' (v.16)

What signs and warnings do we heed? I grew up where seeing black cats, walking under ladders and breaking mirrors were portents of doom; rabbit fur and stepping in dog mess were signs of luck. It took little interpretation. One sign equalled one meaning. There was no need for wisdom, only knowledge, and belief in a mechanistic world where arbitrary signs gave way to unavoidable consequences.

Pharaoh is stumped because his dreams do not follow the usual principles. They call for discernment and wisdom. There is no obvious meaning. As Joseph is called, he does not pretend he can simply recognize a sign and equate it with a consequence. He has to listen to Pharaoh and listen to God. 'It is not I', he says – it is God who gives meaning. The meaning of a dream in God's world is not a warning of unavoidable consequences; the meaning here is a call to prepare, plan and meet the future wisely.

There is a dynamic partnership with God at work, and Joseph has come a long way since his teenage dreams. Instead of dreaming of power, he listens to God on behalf of others in need. This kind of faith is much more demanding than the superstitions of my childhood. How do we nurture this kind of dynamic partnership with God, to discern and respond to the dreams and questions of today?

Holy God,
our lives are laid open before you:
rescue us from the chaos of sin
and through the death of your Son
bring us healing and make us whole
in Jesus Christ our Lord.

COLLECT

Reflection by **Isabelle Hamley**

9

Monday 23 February

Psalms 10, 11 *or* 71
Genesis 41.25-45
Galatians 3.23 – 4.7

Genesis 41.25-45

'God has revealed to Pharaoh' (v.25)

Joseph has undergone a radical transformation. Gone is the self-centred boy who dreams of glory. Instead, the man Joseph, humbled by life's circumstances, exhibits wisdom and concern for those other than himself. He reads the room and knows how to speak to different actors. He is bright, too. He helps Pharaoh, yet knows that Pharaoh can help him, too, and he nonchalantly drops a hint that Pharaoh will need a man of wisdom, having just suggested possible solutions himself!

Joseph has not changed completely: there is still a streak of ambition here and a keen intelligence. But it has been refined and redirected. He has learnt to understand people and work with them. He knows his fate is linked to that of the people who own him. What should he do? There is a dilemma here, behind the story. Working with Pharaoh may bring him freedom; yet working with Pharaoh means working with the empire that owns slaves and arbitrarily puts them in prison for years. Working with Pharaoh will accomplish another goal, too: it will care for the many people of Egypt – and beyond – at a time when death and famine threaten. None of this is brought out clearly in Joseph's story, but our own history of empires and economic oppression begs that we recognize the position that those oppressed by empires and oppressive systems are put in, today as much in history.

COLLECT

Almighty God,
whose Son Jesus Christ fasted forty days in the wilderness,
and was tempted as we are, yet without sin:
give us grace to discipline ourselves in obedience to your Spirit;
and, as you know our weakness,
so may we know your power to save;
through Jesus Christ our Lord.

Reflection by **Isabelle Hamley**

Psalm **44** *or* **73**
Genesis 41.46 – 42.5
Galatians 4.8-20

Tuesday 24 February

Genesis 41.46 – 42.5

'Joseph opened all the storehouses, and sold to the Egyptians'
(41.56)

Joseph has had many years in Egypt, and you can tell. Many years in a place inscribe its culture and values into you. Those of us who have lived in two different countries often find that neither is fully home because too much of each culture permeates who we are. Joseph is a two-cultures person. He still trusts the God of Israel, who cares for all people, is sovereign over nature, and works in partnership with those who believe. Joseph's faith and trust shine through his exclamations about his new life.

Simultaneously, Joseph has become a man of Egypt. Joseph had warned Pharaoh of the coming famine and masterminded heavy levies on grain and goods so that Egypt would be safe during the hungry years. But Joseph was not directed primarily towards the people of Egypt. Joseph was working for Pharaoh's empire. The storehouses are full 'beyond measure' of grain the Egyptian people have produced and given.

When famine hits, Joseph does not simply *give* the grain to the people who had grown and gathered it in the first place. Joseph *sells* the grain and grows Pharaoh's treasure. The land's misfortune has become Pharaoh's opportunity to tighten the grip on his empire. Joseph's imagination is divided, between the God of compassion and the god of empire. The question remains, how do we tell what is shaping our imagination, and which mixed gods we may be serving?

Heavenly Father,
your Son battled with the powers of darkness,
and grew closer to you in the desert:
help us to use these days to grow in wisdom and prayer
that we may witness to your saving love
in Jesus Christ our Lord.

COLLECT

Reflection by **Isabelle Hamley** | 11

Wednesday 25 February

Psalms **6**, 17 *or* **77**
Genesis 42.6-17
Galatians 4.21 – 5.1

Genesis 42.6-17

'... he put them all together in prison for three days' (v.17)

How can you tell what is justice, and what is revenge? And who gets to decide? Joseph was grievously hurt by his brothers. What they did to him was, humanly, unforgiveable. They had hurt a teenage boy and left him to die or be enslaved. They were his brothers and treated him as a stranger, less than human. Joseph had not forgotten. The hurt and trauma now rise to the surface.

What should Joseph do? There was no easy recourse to courts, to safeguarding services, or to any human justice system. What would justice look like anyway in the face of such betrayal of trust and abuse of power?

Power has now been flipped. Joseph is the one with all the power, and his brothers are the vulnerable ones. He can get his own back. He can make them feel exactly as they made him feel. He threatens them and puts them in prison. Is it justice – or revenge?

Most victims have no such power; they do not get to be the powerful one in charge of the fate of those who hurt them. Often, they are left without any recourse to justice. The story of Joseph prompts us to ask how we might nurture communities where survivors can speak up and express the kind of emotions Joseph exhibits through his actions and where we come alongside those seeking justice in the face of intolerable abuse.

COLLECT

Almighty God,
whose Son Jesus Christ fasted forty days in the wilderness,
and was tempted as we are, yet without sin:
give us grace to discipline ourselves in obedience to your Spirit;
and, as you know our weakness,
so may we know your power to save;
through Jesus Christ our Lord.

| *Reflection by* **Isabelle Hamley**

Psalms **42**, 43 *or* **78.1-39***
Genesis 42.18-28
Galatians 5.2-15

Thursday 26 February

Genesis 42.18-28

'... there comes a reckoning' (v.22)

Joseph and his brothers are worlds apart, so far apart that the men do not recognize him. In their minds, he is still the 17-year-old boy they sent into slavery. Time stopped on that day, and they have lived with fear ever since. Joseph's world is still defined by his past, too. He judges his present in the light of his past, and he responds to his brothers, not as the powerful ruler he is, but as a wounded person.

What would be 'right' at this point? Where is God at work? Joseph understood his new position as consolation for his troubles. The brothers think that new threats are a consequence of past actions. They all assume that God is at work in human affairs, but none of them appear to be speaking directly to God, or seeking wisdom and direction from God. Joseph's brothers see the universe as mechanistic and expect punishment from God for wrongdoing, delayed as it may be.

There is little room within their worldviews for grace or forgiveness. Retribution and just desserts rule their imagination of the good and the bad. Yet just desserts rule out grace – and rule out God's freedom, too. At this point of the story, we need to ask, how do God's ways differ from human ways? How do God's justice and restoration differ from human efforts? What might God bring about to break the cycle of human revenge?

Heavenly Father,
your Son battled with the powers of darkness,
and grew closer to you in the desert:
help us to use these days to grow in wisdom and prayer
that we may witness to your saving love
in Jesus Christ our Lord.

COLLECT

Reflection by **Isabelle Hamley**   13

Friday 27 February

Psalm **22** *or* **55**
Genesis 42.29-end
Galatians 5.16-end

Genesis 42.29-end

'... he alone is left' (v.38)

If history teaches us anything, it is that people do not learn from history. We often hope that we can learn for our mistakes, and we hope that children can learn from both their mistakes and from our own too. Human beings, unfortunately, are fickle creatures with strong wills and short memories. We rationalize, make excuses and convince ourselves that today is different.

Jacob was old, old enough to have a lifetime to learn from. He had loved Joseph the most and caused irreparable damage to his family. One would hope he might have learnt, and after losing Joseph, valued his remaining children all the more. He had one more son after Joseph, a son of his old age, and faced with the threat of losing him, refuses compromise, stating 'he alone is left'.

Benjamin is not his only child left. He has many sons, grandsons, daughters and granddaughters. Yet Jacob does not see them. Just as he did with Joseph, he forgets the family he has and puts everyone at risk as a result. Learning takes work; learning from our past needs intentionality and recognition that we get things wrong – and likely will fail to notice the signs next time around. This is why we build habits: confession in our regular worship, keeping Lent every year so we reflect and remember and have a chance of letting our past teach us something to change our future.

COLLECT

Almighty God,
whose Son Jesus Christ fasted forty days in the wilderness,
and was tempted as we are, yet without sin:
give us grace to discipline ourselves in obedience to your Spirit;
and, as you know our weakness,
so may we know your power to save;
through Jesus Christ our Lord.

Reflection by **Isabelle Hamley**

Psalms 59, **63** *or* **76**, 79
Genesis 43.1-15
Galatians 6

Saturday 28 February

Genesis 43.1-15

'Could we in any way know'? (v. 7)

Everyone loves a win–win situation. It is the goal of business, the aim of strategy. Let's find a way forward that gives everyone something of what they want. Jacob had had a lifetime of no-win situations and turned many into 'I win' situations. As a younger brother, he tricked his brother into giving him an elder's birthright; tricked his father into giving him the elder's blessing on his deathbed; tricked his uncle to increase his flock. When trickery wouldn't work, he tried bribery, offering his resources to another. He did this when meeting Esau after their estrangement, and Esau forgave him. Now, faced with another potentially devastating loss, he cannot simply pray, trust, or ask for mercy. Just as with the brothers, grace and freedom are in short supply in his imagination. Therefore, Jacob tries to give what he has to buy mercy.

At this point, no one, possibly not even Joseph, knows whether this is a win–win, a no-win, or a one-win situation. However, within the characters' world, their imagination is so constrained by a graceless universe that it snuffs out the possibility of hope. Hope rests on something beyond human possibilities: God's actions behind the scenes, unforeseen circumstances, and grace where revenge, bitterness and anger are all that can be expected. Hope, grace and imagination go together. In Lent, let us stretch our imaginations so that the possibility of grace can seem a little less far-fetched.

Heavenly Father,
your Son battled with the powers of darkness,
and grew closer to you in the desert:
help us to use these days to grow in wisdom and prayer
that we may witness to your saving love
in Jesus Christ our Lord.

COLLECT

Reflection by **Isabelle Hamley** | 15

Monday 2 March

Genesis 43.16-end

'And they bowed their heads and did obeisance' (v.28)

Sometimes what begins as a dream can end as a nightmare. Life has a way of simply not going how we hope and dream it will go. On other occasions, our initial dreams eventually get achieved, but the path to their fulfilment can be brutal and treacherous, and they make us into complex and sometimes hardened souls.

Joseph is a powerful dreamer, but what we come to understand is that, between the dream and its fulfilment, there is the unthinkable experience of betrayal, first by his brothers, then his master's wife, and then his fellow prisoners. It is Joseph's ability to dream and interpret dreams that sustains him, and his humility and loyalty bring him to the place of highest honour in Pharaoh's kingdom, second only to Pharaoh himself. But what do you do when you come face to face with your betrayers, when the tide has turned, when the ones who tried to kill you now need you for their survival?

In our passage, Joseph accommodates and blesses. Somewhere between the initial dream and its fulfilment, he has found a measure of peace and forgiveness. He yearns for his father and is deeply overjoyed at the sight of his youngest brother, the only other child of his deceased mother. Life can be a harsh journey between our initial dreams and their fulfilment, but God's elevation must be followed by a heart of forgiveness and blessing.

COLLECT

Almighty God,
you show to those who are in error the light of your truth,
that they may return to the way of righteousness:
grant to all those who are admitted
    into the fellowship of Christ's religion,
that they may reject those things
    that are contrary to their profession,
and follow all such things as are agreeable to the same;
through our Lord Jesus Christ.

| *Reflection by* **Carlton Turner**

Psalm **50** *or* 87, **89.1-18**
Genesis 44.1-17
Hebrews 2.1-9

Tuesday 3 March

Genesis 44.1-17

'What can we say to my lord? What can we speak?' (v.16)

Joseph is a trickster with an agenda. He is from a family of tricksters, whose hidden secrets will come to light. Psychological concepts around the 'unconscious' tell us that there is a dimension of ourselves that we're not aware of. It is easy to play games with reality that affect the lives of those around us. Often it is not until we have moments of encounter with the truth that we find ourselves speechless, like Joseph's brothers. Life is often a journey of discovering the truth of who we are, what we've done, and the false desires of our hearts unfolding. These deep things can lie hidden from our consciousness.

In this Lenten season, it is good to reflect on the deeper truths beyond the games we play with ourselves and others. Life has a way of bringing us face to face with our delusions so that we can find new life and freedom. While we play games and orchestrate events and stories for our own sense of control, they eventually lead us to moments where we can only humbly bow and prostrate ourselves before God's truth.

Take a moment this Lent to ask a counsellor, spiritual director or trusted friend to help you examine your blind spots.

Almighty God,
by the prayer and discipline of Lent
may we enter into the mystery of Christ's sufferings,
and by following in his Way
come to share in his glory;
through Jesus Christ our Lord.

COLLECT

Reflection by **Carlton Turner**

Wednesday 4 March

Psalms **35** or **119.105-128**
Genesis 44.18-end
Hebrews 2.10-end

Genesis 44.18-end

'I fear to see the suffering' (v.34)

One of my favourite dictums is 'Time proves all things'. Time has a way of changing us radically. It reveals, often slowly, the implications of our actions in the past. With enough life experience, we come to see how our character changes. Things we would have done in younger years, we dare not repeat in later life. This is the case with Judah. In another life he had been the instigator of a plot to get rid of his brother Joseph. Time has brought him to a similar scenario with his youngest brother, Benjamin. This time, however, he would rather be put into servitude than repeat the same pattern. Time can bring us to the same experiences and challenges at different stages of our lives so that we can see them from different angles.

The yearly pattern of Lenten observance is a good place to take stock of what life has been revealing to us about ourselves, how we view the world, and how we have acted towards those around us. As in our story, it might be that God and time bring us to deep surrender and *metanoia*, the turning of the heart towards God. We begin to realize how much we have grown and changed.

Perhaps, use this time of Lent to express gratitude for all the ways that you have changed as a person. Equally, use this time to mourn all the ways that you have not been godly towards yourself or others.

COLLECT

Almighty God,
you show to those who are in error the light of your truth,
that they may return to the way of righteousness:
grant to all those who are admitted
 into the fellowship of Christ's religion,
that they may reject those things
 that are contrary to their profession,
and follow all such things as are agreeable to the same;
through our Lord Jesus Christ.

| *Reflection by* **Carlton Turner**

Psalm **34** *or* 90, **92**   **Thursday 5 March**
Genesis 45.1-15
Hebrews 3.1-6

Genesis 45.1-15

'I am Joseph' (v.3)

We carry many names throughout our lives. Who we are in relation to others: child, parent/guardian, friend, partner, neighbour and more. Some are for the outside world to give us. We are known by our work or our professional titles, or the pastimes we engage in, even the team we support. Friends and family might have nicknames for us. Colleagues may label us for a particular characteristic. Lovers have their own intimate names for one another. Sometimes our sense of identity can be so shaped by the various roles we fill that our primary sense of identity is forgotten.

For Joseph, it must have been refreshing to finally declare who he was, his name, before the betrayal; before the steward of Potiphar's house; before the dreamer in the prison; and before being second in command to Pharaoh. It must have been healing to declare his name, his truth, and to be seen and known in return.

Lent can be a time when we come to seek who we truly are in the midst of an often harsh world. The spiritual writer Henri Nouwen said that knowing ourselves as God's 'Beloved' is perhaps the most surprising knowledge of all. Yet, this is the primary and only name given by God to a lost and fallen humanity. Can you remember when you got to hear your name said to you as only a parent can? Today take a moment to hear the tender call of the lover God, calling you by your name. How will you respond?

Almighty God,
by the prayer and discipline of Lent
may we enter into the mystery of Christ's sufferings,
and by following in his Way
come to share in his glory;
through Jesus Christ our Lord.

COLLECT

Reflection by **Carlton Turner**   19

Friday 6 March

Psalms 40, **41** *or* **88** (95)
Genesis 45.16-end
Hebrews 3.7-end

Genesis 45.16-end

'... the spirit of their father Jacob revived' (v.27)

I am fortunate to have had the chance to know my great-grandmother, who died at the age of 95. She was quite a character. Knowing her helped me make sense of my grandmother, and then my mother. They all live within me, and their stories and unique characteristics have shaped who I am. Revival, literally coming alive again, is not a gift granted to many. The more I live and experience life, especially as a priest, I see how many lives are cut short.

Because of the mobility of modern life, families often live far apart, and grandparents do not always get to meet their grandchildren to pass on their stories. Families and relationships become disrupted by so many trials: isolation, separation, poverty, illness and death. It is increasingly rare that we hold onto memories of our forebears, that they get to be 'revived' in our own lives. While Jacob, in all the complexity of his journey, gets to be revived upon learning of Joseph being alive, Rachel, Joseph's mother, did not get to see this great day.

The chance to be revived, to be pleasantly surprised, and to see the eventual working of justice is a gift denied to many. Lent is a time to rejoice both in good fortune and in grace. But it is also a sobering time to remember the misfortunes of others. When have you had bittersweet moments like this? What do they bring to new life within you?

COLLECT

Almighty God,
you show to those who are in error the light of your truth,
that they may return to the way of righteousness:
grant to all those who are admitted
into the fellowship of Christ's religion,
that they may reject those things
that are contrary to their profession,
and follow all such things as are agreeable to the same;
through our Lord Jesus Christ.

Saturday 7 March

Genesis 46.1-7, 28-end

'I am God, the God of your father' (v.3)

There are pieces of music that have followed me throughout my life, giving me comfort, especially in times of crisis or when I'm at a crossroads – for example, 'Broken Wings' by 1980s rock band Mr. Mister. Meaningful songs like this one always signal to me that God is near, and that the one who had known me as a teenager, seen me through my 20s and 30s, is still with me in my mid-40s. At times, these experiences are quite powerful as reminders of God's enduring presence.

We see something of this in the life of Jacob, who hears the words echoed to him when he first ran away from his father's house and from the wrath of his brother Esau (Genesis 28). Sometimes God has a way of having his words and promises come back to us, often through familiar scriptures uttered at the right time, or through art, music, or the counsel of friends. These are also part of our journeys in life.

What particular moments can you recall where you sensed God's presence and assurance? What impact did they have on you? How did they deepen your faith? More importantly, what were these moments pointing towards? For those without such experiences – since not everyone has them – how do you sustain your faith during life's circumstances? Lent is a time for remembering and introspection for us all.

Almighty God,
by the prayer and discipline of Lent
may we enter into the mystery of Christ's sufferings,
and by following in his Way
come to share in his glory;
through Jesus Christ our Lord.

COLLECT

Reflection by **Carlton Turner**

21

Monday 9 March

Genesis 47.1-27
'Give us food!' (v.15)

It is a privilege to live in a country where food is plentiful. Access to food is so bountiful in the West that tons get thrown away every day. While there are people and communities struggling with poverty and hunger in Western nations, the reality of what a real famine is is unimaginable for us. In many other parts of the world, famine and drought are day-to-day realities. Often these situations are further exacerbated by conflict and war. Famine is not simply a problem about the lack of food. It is also about political power, who controls economic resources, and whether those who have both are willing to share them to help the most vulnerable and marginalized.

Joseph is a shrewd manager. He has power, second only to Pharaoh's. He devises a skilful trade strategy that gives Pharaoh total control of the land. In a time of famine, people exchanged their lands and their livelihoods for food. This led to them being enslaved to Pharaoh. This is not an easy passage to grasp. Sometimes the most abused and downtrodden can become skilled despots. This capitalistic Joseph is not who we expect, and we can read this passage with naive eyes. We must be careful with how we use power, and at whose expense power and wealth are accumulated. Lent is a reminder to pray for deliverance from the idolatry of money and power that takes advantage of the poor and the vulnerable in our world.

C O L L E C T

Almighty God,
whose most dear Son went not up to joy
    but first he suffered pain,
and entered not into glory before he was crucified:
mercifully grant that we, walking in the way of the cross,
may find it none other than the way of life and peace;
through Jesus Christ our Lord.

| *Reflection by* **Carlton Turner**

Psalms 6, **9** *or* **106*** *(or* 103)
Genesis 47.28 – end of 48
Hebrews 5.11 – 6.12

Tuesday 10 March

Genesis 47.28 – end of 48

'Do not bury me in Egypt' (47.29)

I've presided at many funerals of people who insisted on coming back to their home parish to be buried. They might have lived in different parts of the country for decades, but it mattered that their final resting place was where they were raised and where their parents and siblings were buried.

This resonates with me. My life has taken me from a rural island in the Bahamas to the bustling West Midlands of England. I have invested much time and energy and made fond memories in both places. But home is special. The little graveyard where my great-grandparents are buried means a lot to me. The little church I grew up in is also where I was ordained deacon. It is my deepest and most enduring sense of home.

Jacob is dying. He wishes to be buried with his ancestors. The irony of these deep longings is that we often function best where we are because we have a sense of a home to return to. While Egypt is a place where he could sing his songs and where everything seems to have turned out well in the end, it is still not home. It is not the place where he first knew of God; where he first fell in love; where his heart still lay.

Where is your deepest sense of home, or what forms your deepest sense of identity?

Eternal God,
give us insight
to discern your will for us,
to give up what harms us,
and to seek the perfection we are promised
in Jesus Christ our Lord.

COLLECT

Reflection by **Carlton Turner** | 23

Wednesday 11 March

Psalm **38** *or* 110, 111, 112
Genesis 49.1-32
Hebrews 6.13-end

Genesis 49.1-32

'Gather around' (v. 1)

The ancient rite of blessing one's children before death is seen in many cultures around the world, particularly more ancient and indigenous ones. Death and departure are not individualistic moments; they are important for the extended community's sense of history, of continuity. As a child, I remembered that families and friends would gather around to hear the last words of their loved ones and mourn together when they passed away. There was something sacred about this. And, while much of our loved ones' wishes are written into wills and legal documents, there is still something so important about words of blessing. Mike and the Mechanic's iconic song, 'The Living Years', with its theme of regret for things left unsaid is a good reminder here of the importance of speaking to and with our loved ones before they pass away.

Jacob has a chance to bless his children and speak into their lives. He expresses his wishes clearly, but he also touches and blesses his sons and their children. He entrusts them to the God of his ancestors. This gathering around to be blessed is not just for the familial community but is part of the divine community. He and his descendants are part of God's story, an unbreakable bond between heaven and earth.

Lent is a time when we can utter words of blessing or seek to gather our loved ones together before God, entrusting them to God's future. This is a sacred act.

COLLECT

Almighty God,
whose most dear Son went not up to joy
    but first he suffered pain,
and entered not into glory before he was crucified:
mercifully grant that we, walking in the way of the cross,
may find it none other than the way of life and peace;
through Jesus Christ our Lord.

| *Reflection by* **Carlton Turner**

Psalms **56**, 57 *or* 113, **115**   **Thursday 12 March**
Genesis 49.33 – end of 50
Hebrews 7.1-10

Genesis 49.33 – end of 50

'When the days of weeping for him were past' (50.4)

Life is not complete without its weeping. Tears can express what words are incapable of achieving for they are complex and speak of the deep experiences of the soul and the heart. They can be tears of pain, tears of healing, tears of relief, tears of anger, or tears of laughter and joy. Whatever their cause, they point to deep love and connection. They are part of what it means to be human. We live in a world that is increasingly more automated and less empathetic. Systems of power and control so often act inhumanely without any sense of sympathy or compassion.

Just imagine for a moment the many tears of Joseph as he mourns his father's death. One can wonder about many years of separation; the unspeakable joy of reconnecting again; and then the equally unspeakable grief of losing him again. These are complex tears, and the entire community weeps with him.

Lent is a time when we can face our weeping and allow our tears to flow. It is a time to remember that we are human, with deep capacity for love and connection. In this holy season, we can attend to the deeply unresolved parts of our story, seeking opportunities to notice them, feel them and honour them. However, as Lent must end, so does the time of weeping. May we get up from our time of weeping to be stronger human beings before God and others.

Eternal God,
give us insight
to discern your will for us,
to give up what harms us,
and to seek the perfection we are promised
in Jesus Christ our Lord.

COLLECT

Reflection by **Carlton Turner**   25

Friday 13 March

Exodus 1.1-14

'Now a new king arose over Egypt' (v.8)

I'm always amazed at how the tables can turn in life. In foreign policy and international diplomacy, a country that was an ally in one period of history becomes an absolute enemy in another. These turns of fortune mark our lived existence in history, if we live long enough to see it. Some of these happen quickly. In our friendships and close relationships, we go through phases and moments where much is disrupted and what was normal is turned upside down. These experiences are traumatic, and no one is immune to them.

In today's reading, we come to a new phase in the journey of the Hebrews. They were once beloved and cherished. Now they are despised and envied. A new pharaoh rises to the throne who does not know of Joseph and does not remember the great blessing this Hebrew figure brought to the land. Often at the heart of turns of fortune or changes in relationships is the inability to remember the bigger story or the longer history. In fact, forgetting or ignoring our shared story and our complex interdependence is often what brings about the turn of fortune in the first place.

Lent is a time for remembering and moving beyond dualistic thinking that makes one side the victim and the other the villain. Lent helps us to see that our shared story is much more complex and more hopeful than we dare to think.

COLLECT

Almighty God,
whose most dear Son went not up to joy
    but first he suffered pain,
and entered not into glory before he was crucified:
mercifully grant that we, walking in the way of the cross,
may find it none other than the way of life and peace;
through Jesus Christ our Lord.

Reflection by **Carlton Turner**

Psalm **31** *or* 120, **121**, 122
Exodus 1.22 – 2.10
Hebrews 8

Saturday 14 March

Exodus 1.22 – 2.10

'She named him Moses' (2.10)

There is something about the story of Moses that speaks of baptism. In baptism, we are given a name to signify our identity in Jesus Christ as the beloved children of God, belonging to the beloved family of God. We are also plunged into waters as a ritual cleansing and raised up as a renewed people. Through the mystery of baptism, we are given new life and a new destiny.

For many of us in our comfortable Christian congregations, this can all be symbolic and ritualistic. We are fortunate to live our Christian lives in relative peace and tranquillity. But, Moses, who is drawn from the waters, doesn't enjoy such comforts. His story is set in a world of infanticide, bloodshed, anguish and trauma. Moses' life is spared through trickery and out of utter desperation.

Here is a story of a people caught up in a violent ruling system and slave labour, yet whose cries of lament are heard in heaven. The child saved from the waters becomes the one who brings deliverance through the waters of the Red Sea. Lent reminds us of the cost of our baptism and our calling to live for the transformation of the world. Many people today are living under the oppressive systems of the world. We hear their cries and work for their rescue because we have been drawn from the waters.

Eternal God,
give us insight
to discern your will for us,
to give up what harms us,
and to seek the perfection we are promised
in Jesus Christ our Lord.

COLLECT

Reflection by **Carlton Turner**

27

Monday 16 March Psalms 70, **77** *or* 123, 124, 125, **126**
Exodus 2.11-22
Hebrews 9.1-14

Exodus 2.11-22

'He settled in the land of Midian, and sat down by a well' (v.15)

Moses' name means 'drawn out of the water', and water features prominently in his story – crossing the Red Sea, water gushing from the rock he strikes. He's fluid, not a fixed element. Moses goes through a huge identity crisis. Brought up an Egyptian, he discovers his 'Hebrewness'. Simultaneously his old life implodes, and he must flee to find a resting place with a third ethnic group: the Midianites.

The early chapters of Exodus do not show any of these groups as uniformly good or bad. One of the fighting Hebrews is in the wrong, and his denunciation of Moses is what turns Moses into a refugee. Some of the Midianites show immense hospitality to this foreigner, while others (the shepherds from whom Moses rescues Jethro's daughters) are thugs.

Perhaps Moses himself is on a journey in relation to such complexities of identity. His killing of the Egyptian who's beating a Hebrew is based on a simple sense of ethnic solidarity. He instinctively defends his kin. His shock that two Hebrews should be fighting one another is based on the same instinct. But in Midian, at an early example of what will be many wells in the biblical story (they are the dating site of the ancient near-Middle East!), things change. Nowhere and everywhere can be home when your God is the God of the whole world; and anyone can be your kin, like poured water adapting to whatever vessels God has chosen for it.

C O L L E C T | Merciful Lord,
absolve your people from their offences,
that through your bountiful goodness
we may all be delivered from the chains of those sins
which by our frailty we have committed;
grant this, heavenly Father,
for Jesus Christ's sake, our blessed Lord and Saviour.

| *Reflection by* **Ben Quash**

Psalms 54, **79** *or* **132**, 133
Exodus 2.23 – 3.20
Hebrews 9.15-end

Tuesday 17 March

Exodus 2.23 – 3.20

'I must turn aside and look ...' (3.3)

Moses' encounter with the burning bush is a quintessential example of a double take.

First, he sees the bush, and then he *goes over and looks* at it – a second looking that involves him in turning aside from his intended path. This reminds me of the distinction between 'seeing' and 'looking' drawn by the art critic Roger Fry, writing in 1919. Seeing, he says, has to do with the use that appearances have for the business of living. It is functional. We extract key information as rapidly as possible from this kind of seeing. It tells whether the movement in the long grass is the wind or a tiger about to pounce; whether the bread has gone mouldy. Looking, however, is a type of vision that is 'quite distinct from the practical vision of our instinctive life', he argues. When we *look*, our vision 'dwells much more consciously and deliberately' upon the object in front of us. Fry thinks children have a special capacity for this. They look at things, he says, with '*passion*'.

Moses stops, reorients himself and *really looks*. This is no longer just the gathering of visual information. Once he has turned aside to look, the voice of God can really address him. Moses takes his sandals off, prostrates himself and is transformed. It is now a moment of relationship.

Merciful Lord,
you know our struggle to serve you:
when sin spoils our lives
and overshadows our hearts,
come to our aid
and turn us back to you again;
through Jesus Christ our Lord.

COLLECT

Wednesday 18 March

Psalms 63, **90** or **119.153-end**
Exodus 4.1-23
Hebrews 10.1-18

Exodus 4.1-23

'... when he took it out, it was restored' (v.7)

'The Lord kills and brings to life' (1 Samuel 2.6). We see such power vividly displayed in the three signs Moses and Aaron are told to enact, to prove that they are doing God's work. A wooden staff becomes a snake; a healthy hand becomes leprous; and (should a third sign be needed) water will become dried blood. Snake's venom, disease and spilt blood. All these are signs of death – perhaps also, therefore, premonitions of the great plagues to come.

Then – as Moses is instructed to grasp the snake's tail and to put his hand inside his cloak a second time – God shows that what he takes away he can give back just as easily. Restoration to the *status quo ante* (to how things were before) is a marvellous thing. Many of Jesus' miracles achieved just this and brought great joy – perhaps most dramatically in the raising of Lazarus. But Jesus revealed greater wonders even than these in his ministry, when things became *more* than they were before. Water into wine; fishermen into disciples; and earthly life into risen glory. Revivification is not the same as resurrection (though it may be a sign of it). Resurrection opens a new pathway.

So with Moses. The miracles of the restored staff and the restored hand return things to how they were before. But a greater miracle is presaged here. Slavery will become freedom; a people with no home will be given one.

COLLECT

Merciful Lord,
absolve your people from their offences,
that through your bountiful goodness
we may all be delivered from the chains of those sins
which by our frailty we have committed;
grant this, heavenly Father,
for Jesus Christ's sake, our blessed Lord and Saviour.

| *Reflection by* **Ben Quash**

Psalms 25, 147.1-12
Isaiah 11.1-10
Matthew 13.54-end

Thursday 19 March
Joseph of Nazareth

Isaiah 11.1-10
'... for the meek of the earth' (v.4)

'If there is one place where our century needs to understand the meaning of meekness, it is behind the wheel of an automobile', wrote the American author and journalist Sherwood Wirt in 1964. The biblical scholar Rebekah Eklund adds that, in the twenty-first century, social media might have a similar claim.

But what is meekness? We've come to think of it as a weak virtue, evoking shyness, proneness to intimidation and a lack of self-assertion. Understood like that, we may find it strange that the meek are commended by Isaiah, while in the same verse he also celebrates strength: 'he shall strike the earth with the rod of his mouth'.

Our lacklustre picture of meekness is a modern invention. For most of history, the meek have been identified as those with the ability to temper their strength appropriately. Because they are not subject to uncontrolled emotion, the meek know when to be angry, how to be angry, and for how long to be angry. By the same token, they know when and how to yield: to turn the other cheek to their neighbours and to bow their knee to God.

It makes sense that in a redeemed world Isaiah shows us mighty animals acting with perfect self-control. Their meekness is a quality not of the powerless but of the powerful.

It takes strength to be truly gentle.

God our Father,
who from the family of your servant David
raised up Joseph the carpenter
to be the guardian of your incarnate Son
and husband of the Blessed Virgin Mary:
give us grace to follow him
in faithful obedience to your commands;
through Jesus Christ our Lord.

COLLECT

Reflection by **Ben Quash**   31

Friday 20 March

Psalm **102** *or* 142, **144**
Exodus 6.2-13
Hebrews 10.26-end

Exodus 6.2-13

'... by my name "The Lord" I did not make myself known to them'
(v.3)

The infinitely mysterious and full name of God disclosed to Moses at the burning bush – 'I AM THAT I AM' (Exodus 3.14) – is here evoked again by God in what will hereafter be its abbreviated form: YHWH. The resolutely peculiar Hebrew of this name is notoriously difficult to translate. The tense of the verb *ehyeh* has a futural implication that the most common English translation 'I AM' does not capture; it suggests not so much a static state of merely subsisting as a dynamic state of coming to pass. This is not a God whose meaning may be possessed, nor whose actions may be predicted simply on the basis of already-given states of affairs.

God says that he withheld this name from Abraham, Isaac and Jacob, Moses' forebears. But they were on the way to it. According to an ancient Jewish midrashic story, Abraham's (then still called Abram) great journey of faith began when he took a stick and smashed the idols in his father Terah's idol shop, except the largest one, which he left holding the stick. When Terah arrived on the scene, Abram blamed the destruction on the idol. 'But he's just a statue!', says Terah. 'Precisely', says Abram. What Abraham began to discern back then, Moses now has confirmed to him in this name. In its refusal to be tamed, its call to leave behind the little gods of our own making, it's a name that sets God's people free.

COLLECT

Merciful Lord,
absolve your people from their offences,
that through your bountiful goodness
we may all be delivered from the chains of those sins
which by our frailty we have committed;
grant this, heavenly Father,
for Jesus Christ's sake, our blessed Lord and Saviour.

| *Reflection by* **Ben Quash**

Psalms **32** *or* **147**
Exodus 7.8-end
Hebrews 11.1-16

Saturday 21 March

Exodus 7.8-end

'... and it [the Nile] shall be turned to blood' (v.17)

In the Bible, and in so many human cultures, water is a powerful symbol for life itself: the life that makes our world fertile. We need clean, fresh water, and we need it in abundance, so that the earth may flourish, and so that we may flourish along with it. And because God is the source of our life – because he made us and sustains us – God is sometimes compared with water. We might think of a prophecy of the Old Testament prophet Hosea, who has a wonderful image of God watering the earth by the gift of his own self, so that it may be fruitful: 'I will be like the dew to Israel' (Hosea 14.5).

But water is not the only liquid symbol for life in the Bible. So is blood. 'The blood is the life' (Deuteronomy 12.23) that courses through our veins. When life ebbs away from Jesus Christ on the cross, it does so in the form of blood and water.

In this first plague, however, blood is where water should be. Just as what we call 'dirt' is often something capable of being useful except for the fact that it has turned up in the wrong place – and what a parent calls 'mud' on a child's sports kit is something a gardener would call 'soil' – so this blood has transgressed its bounds. It points to other transgressions – Pharaoh's – which also have death as their consequence.

COLLECT

Merciful Lord,
you know our struggle to serve you:
when sin spoils our lives
and overshadows our hearts,
come to our aid
and turn us back to you again;
through Jesus Christ our Lord.

Monday 23 March

Exodus 8.1-19

'... the magicians did the same by their secret arts' (v.7)

It is a part of the self-destructiveness of human nature that we prize our self-justification over what would manifestly be the best outcome. We dig in. We will be proved right even if it kills us.

Pharaoh's magicians see Egypt overwhelmed by a seething mass of frogs. It is catastrophic for their land and their people. The solution before them, and their master, is plain and clear: 'Let my people go.' But they are locked in a competitive cycle of disastrous wonder-mongering. So *they* make frogs too. They compound the misery they and their master have brought on themselves. They'll be damned if they give up now – though, of course, they are being damned for quite the opposite reason.

The stubbornness of the human heart may also account for Pharaoh's delay when Moses asks him when he should ask God to end the frog invasion. 'Tomorrow', says Pharaoh. What purpose is that extra 24 hours of horror, other than to massage an ego, and nurse resentment? Such stubbornness cannot ultimately prevail. Little by little, the limits of its negative power are being exposed, and when the gnats descend, the magicians concede defeat: '[they] tried to produce gnats by their secret arts, but they could not'. There has been so much avoidable attrition. But Pharaoh is nowhere near being ready to end this arms race yet.

COLLECT

Most merciful God,
who by the death and resurrection of your Son Jesus Christ
delivered and saved the world:
grant that by faith in him who suffered on the cross
we may triumph in the power of his victory;
through Jesus Christ our Lord.

Reflection by **Ben Quash**

Psalms **35**, 123 *or* **5**, 6 (8)
Exodus 8.20-end
Hebrews 11.32 – 12.2

Exodus 8.20-end

'But Pharaoh hardened his heart this time also ...' (v.32)

The matter of Pharaoh's hardened heart has long preoccupied those with an interest in free will. This is because, throughout the early chapters of Exodus, two things are regularly reiterated: the Lord hardened Pharaoh's heart, and Pharaoh hardened his own heart.

St Augustine argued we are not taking anything away from Pharaoh's free will if in some passages God says 'I have hardened Pharoah'. For 'it does not by any means follow that Pharaoh did not, on this account, harden his own heart':

> For this, too, is said of him, after the removal of the fly-plague from the Egyptians [...]: 'And Pharaoh hardened his heart at this time also; neither would he let the people go.' Thus it was that both God hardened him by his just judgment, and Pharaoh by his own free will. (*On Grace and Free Will*)

Perhaps the issue here is not who has their hands on the controls of Pharaoh's actions: a competitive model of divine and human agency, in which an increase in one automatically entails a decrease in the other. Perhaps, on the contrary, God is (in Augustine's word) 'forsaking' Pharaoh, rather than forcing anything on him. And in this lessening of God's grace, Pharaoh's agency is diminished too. As Augustine also said, he becomes more and more stuck in his 'most iniquitous and malignant obstinacy'.

Where God is active, we are all the more activated. Where God withdraws, our own human capacities atrophy.

Gracious Father,
you gave up your Son
out of love for the world:
lead us to ponder the mysteries of his passion,
that we may know eternal peace
through the shedding of our Saviour's blood,
Jesus Christ our Lord.

COLLECT

Reflection by **Ben Quash** | 35

Wednesday 25 March

Annunciation of Our Lord
to the Blessed Virgin Mary

Psalms 111, 113
1 Samuel 2.1-10
Romans 5.12-end

1 Samuel 2.1-10

'Hannah prayed ...' (v.1)

To whom is this prayer directed? Who is meant to hear it?

In many ways, it is a powerful description of the sort of God that God is. And for the most part it seems to be spoken more *about* God than *to* God. In this it has much in common with its sister prayer, uttered centuries later: Mary's Magnificat. Indeed, it seems that a very human audience to the prayer is presupposed by Hannah, as she derides those who derided her in her childlessness: 'Talk no more so very proudly, let not arrogance come from your mouth.' Nevertheless, a second-person address to God also breaks the surface in verse 2. After Hannah has exclaimed 'There is no Holy One like the Lord', she adds 'no one besides you'. So, God is undoubtedly an auditor, too.

Many of the great prayers of the Christian tradition assume a double audience in this way. Augustine's *Confessions* is a book-length prayer to God, written to be 'overheard' by others. And so it has been – with immense spiritual profit – by generations of later readers.

This is because the relationship with God from which prayer springs is communal, even when we pray alone. The theologians of the early Church saw in Hannah's prayer the prayer of the City of God itself: the Church that is 'full of grace', fruitful in spiritual children – the Church in which Mary, too, prays.

COLLECT

We beseech you, O Lord,
pour your grace into our hearts,
that as we have known the incarnation of your Son Jesus Christ
    by the message of an angel,
so by his cross and passion
we may be brought to the glory of his resurrection;
through Jesus Christ our Lord.

Psalms **40**, 125 *or* 14, **15**, 16
Exodus 9.13-end
Hebrews 12.14-end

Thursday 26 March

Exodus 9.13-end

*'... so that you may know that there is no one like me
in all the earth' (v.14)*

The ten plagues can be read in conjunction with the creation narratives in the book of Genesis. They are like a terrible inversion of all that God accomplished in making the world. They are like 'uncreation'. We learn that 'there is no other like God in all the earth' from God's power to create. Now Pharaoh (and we, with our own hardened hearts?) are invited to learn the same lesson in witnessing God's power to unravel what once was knitted together so beautifully.

God separated things out in creation (heaven from earth; land from sea), whereas here things overspill their apportioned limits. God made the waters teem with fish, whereas here the fish suffocate in blood. God made the land abundant with plant and animal life, but here, a hail comes that destroys not only the beasts of the field, but also the crops and the trees. The few plants that survive the hail will not be able to escape the locusts that come next.

Finally, there will be the undoing of what was created before anything else was made: all will be returned to darkness.

The plagues are a mixture of surfeit and privation. A multiplication of frogs and insects; a subtraction of health (in pestilence and boils) and, ultimately, of light. It is both the excess and the meanness in our dealings with one another and with the non-human world that are mirrored here.

Most merciful God,
who by the death and resurrection of your Son Jesus Christ
delivered and saved the world:
grant that by faith in him who suffered on the cross
we may triumph in the power of his victory;
through Jesus Christ our Lord.

COLLECT

Reflection by **Ben Quash**   37

Friday 27 March

Psalms **22**, 126 *or* 17, **19**
Exodus 10
Hebrews 13.1-16

Exodus 10

'... on the day you see my face you shall die' (v.28)

Why would the king of the most powerful nation on earth agree to liberate his slave population merely because a turncoat subject asks him to? He wouldn't. But the request comes from one greater than Moses. This is a battle for sovereignty. Moses and Aaron carry a staff in which God's authority is vested. They can pass it between them; they do not cling to its power. Byzantine emperors would later have the symbol of the 'staff of Moses' carried before them during solemn processions, to signify their answerability to God as legislators and rulers.

But Pharaoh is jealous of God's authority, and he exercises *his* will in an attempt to overcome *God's* will that the Hebrews be liberated: to thwart Israel's mission in God's plan. It is a huge irony that Pharaoh's words to Moses as he banishes him from his presence are an echo of words that belong properly only to God: 'no one shall see me and live' (Exodus 33.20).

Maybe the Bible is inviting us to hear this echo as revealing of Pharaoh's god-like pretensions. Yet he appears more and more isolated, as first his magicians and then his officials have ceased to stand with him: 'do you not yet understand that Egypt is ruined?' He will not hear what Israel hears: 'The Lord is God, the Lord alone' (Deuteronomy 6.4)

COLLECT

Most merciful God,
who by the death and resurrection of your Son Jesus Christ
delivered and saved the world:
grant that by faith in him who suffered on the cross
we may triumph in the power of his victory;
through Jesus Christ our Lord.

| *Reflection by* **Ben Quash**

Psalms **23**, 127 *or* 20, 21, **23**
Exodus 11
Hebrews 13.17-end

Saturday 28 March

Exodus 11

'Every firstborn in the land of Egypt shall die' (v.5)

Pharaoh has made tiny concession after tiny concession as the successive plagues hit. But never enough. Time has run out. The undoing of creation's various goods in plague upon plague will now envelop human life itself on a cataclysmic scale. In the slaughter of the firstborn, all differences of wealth and social station are eradicated, even the difference between humans and other animals: 'from the firstborn of Pharaoh [...] to the firstborn of the female slave [...] and all the firstborn of the livestock'.

One difference remains – so stark that even the dogs on the street recognize it. It is that between Egypt and Israel: God's rejecters and God's elect. The contrast between Egypt and Israel encoded in this story can be a dangerous one because it is so easy to insert ourselves into it as though we are the chosen ones, and to identify ever-new Pharaohs who are our enemies. Christians can do that whenever they claim that they are the ones whom God now protects. And we have sometimes made Jews pay the price for our attempt to find a home in this world as (metaphorically) we paint Jesus' blood on our lintels.

If we have sometimes 'become Pharaoh' to Jews, then it is also true that the dangers run in all directions. Jews can become Pharaoh to Muslims, and Muslims to Christians. We are all called to perpetual vigilance for our hardness of heart.

Gracious Father,
you gave up your Son
out of love for the world:
lead us to ponder the mysteries of his passion,
that we may know eternal peace
through the shedding of our Saviour's blood,
Jesus Christ our Lord.

COLLECT

Reflection by **Ben Quash**　39

Monday 30 March
Monday of Holy Week

Psalm 41
Lamentations 1.1-12*a*
Luke 22.1-23

Lamentations 1.1-12*a*
'Look and see' (v.12)

This passage in Lamentations paints a picture of utter desolation, and the bleakness of present existence is even more excruciating in the remembering of how things had been so different in the past. There was once a time of privilege and celebration, but now that has all changed and there is a sense of having been discarded. The pain is exacerbated by the situation seemingly not being recognized by those around.

Our personal experiences of the present in the light of the past may or may not resonate with these verses, but as we live these days of Holy Week, may these verses provoke us to stop and look. To take time to look and see deep within our hearts and minds amid our present story, and to look more broadly across our local context and the wider world. To look with honesty at our brokenness and that of the world, and not to pass it by.

Holy Week invites us to carry all that we see to the foot of the cross so that we might look on the face of Christ and see the overwhelming, inexplicable love of God in more profound ways than before and reach out to receive that love from the God who looks and sees and does not pass by.

COLLECT

Almighty and everlasting God,
who in your tender love towards the human race
    sent your Son our Saviour Jesus Christ
to take upon him our flesh
and to suffer death upon the cross:
grant that we may follow the example of his patience and humility,
and also be made partakers of his resurrection;
through Jesus Christ our Lord.

   Reflection by **Rachel Treweek**

Psalm 27
Lamentations 3.1-18
Luke 22. [24-38] 39-53

Tuesday 31 March
Tuesday of Holy Week

Lamentations 3.1-18
'... I call and cry for help' (v.8)

These very personal words of the writer encompass the pain and brokenness of the entire world, past and present. This week we will once again face the unfathomable truth that God's love for the world is revealed in Jesus Christ's torturous and humiliating death, and it is not hard to imagine Christ recalling these words from Lamentations as he cried out: 'My God, my God why have you forsaken me?' (Mark 15.34).

Today, many echo the writer's cries of bitterness and tribulation: those who are walled in with no obvious path of escape, perhaps in homes where there is abuse, or in countries under siege; those experiencing a sense of deep darkness without any sign of light; and many crying out for help but feeling unheard. All of these and more may have an overwhelming sense of God's absence. It is sometimes tempting to rush to words of hope and resurrection rather than dwelling with the pain and the lament.

Today, how can you stretch your heart and mind to see and feel the sorrows of the world close by and far away (and not only in the media headlines) and to cry out to God with those words of the psalmist 'How long, O Lord?' (Psalm 13.1).

COLLECT

True and humble king,
hailed by the crowd as Messiah:
grant us the faith to know you and love you,
that we may be found beside you
on the way of the cross,
which is the path of glory.

Reflection by **Rachel Treweek** | 41

Wednesday 1 April
Wednesday of Holy Week

Psalm 102 [*or* 102.1-18]
Wisdom 1.16 – 2.1; 2.12-22
or Jeremiah 11.18-20
Luke 22.54-end

Jeremiah 11.18-20

'... to you I have committed my cause' (v.20)

Jeremiah's words reflect a deep and dark hostility emanating from those around him. As power is wielded by powerful opponents combining forces and using deceit in their intent to utterly destroy and silence, Jeremiah's cries are heartfelt and determined.

A desire for justice is good and right, yet justice is a complex matter; sometimes our thirst for it abandons mercy and gets entangled with an understandable desire for vengeance. These verses are a reminder that we can be honest with God as we pour out our visceral emotions and thoughts, while being willing to let go and commit our cause to God whose ways are beyond ours.

In this Holy Week, we cannot fail to be aware of the hostility Jesus Christ experienced in his earthly life, particularly as the events resulting in his crucifixion unfolded, yet he stood resolute in the face of cruel injustice.

When we feel wronged or perceive injustice in the lives of others, it is honest to rage and lament while remembering that God is the only one who truly sees and that Holy Week points to the truth that one day justice will be restored through Christ in whom all things hold together (Colossians 1.17).

C
O
L
L
E
C
T

Almighty and everlasting God,
who in your tender love towards the human race
    sent your Son our Saviour Jesus Christ
to take upon him our flesh
and to suffer death upon the cross:
grant that we may follow the example of his patience and humility,
and also be made partakers of his resurrection;
through Jesus Christ our Lord.

Reflection by **Rachel Treweek**

Psalms 42, 43
Leviticus 16.2-24
Luke 23.1-25

Thursday 2 April
Maundy Thursday

Leviticus 16.2-24

'... because of the uncleannesses of the people' (v.16)

These detailed and complex instructions regarding Aaron's priestly ritual of atonement are marked each year by our Jewish brothers and sisters on the annual Day of Atonement; these verses are full of phrases that have echoed down the years in Christian doctrine and worship – for example, the mercy seat that signifies God's presence, and the concept of being washed clean as a metaphor for forgiveness. Furthermore, we see the goat on which all the sins of the people are laid, which gives rise to the term 'scapegoat'.

This passage is pertinent as we stand on the threshold of Good Friday, when we will recall Christ's sacrificial death. Many churches today will re-enact the Last Supper and the washing of feet, reminding us again of Christ's self-offering as he prepares to give himself up to death for the forgiveness of sins and out of love for the whole world.

God's instructions to Moses can appear stark and almost clinical, and the mystery and wonder of God's forgiveness can be lost amid the need to explain and analyse. Instead, today may we immerse ourselves in the depths of God's love and forgiveness, giving thanks for God's inexplicable mercy, God's desire to remove our sins far from us, so that, like the goat released into the wilderness, we are wholly free of them.

COLLECT

True and humble king,
hailed by the crowd as Messiah:
grant us the faith to know you and love you,
that we may be found beside you
on the way of the cross,
which is the path of glory.

Reflection by **Rachel Treweek**

Friday 3 April
Good Friday

Psalm 69
Genesis 22.1-18
Hebrews 10.1-10

Genesis 22.1-18
'Here I am' (v.1)

This harrowing episode of Abraham being willing to sacrifice his son in obedience to God is deeply disturbing. It is right for a child to trust their parents and to expect their protection, and it is right that we are distressed when this is not the case. Furthermore, our faith is rooted in God whose parental love is unfailing, so how could God engender such a traumatic experience in the life of a family?

Yet, if we resist the temptation to try and rationalize every detail of this passage, making it more comfortable, our outrage may enable us to engage more deeply with the disturbing narrative and unanswered questions surrounding this holy day.

On this day we recall Jesus Christ, the son of God, strung up on a cross and tortured to death. There is no last-minute rescue, yet we name this Friday as 'Good'. We cannot explain this perplexing and ultimate act of God's self-giving love, but like Abraham speaking first to God and then to his son, we too can say 'Here I am'. As we remain present and open to God and to those around us in all that perturbs, angers, distresses and confuses us, let us stand at the foot of the cross offering ourselves to God and seeking to be incomprehensibly transformed. 'Here I am.'

COLLECT

Almighty Father,
look with mercy on this your family
for which our Lord Jesus Christ was content to be betrayed
    and given up into the hands of sinners
    and to suffer death upon the cross;
who is alive and glorified with you and the Holy Spirit,
one God, now and for ever.

*Reflection by **Rachel Treweek***

Psalm 142
Hosea 6.1-6
John 2.18-22

Saturday 4 April
Easter Eve

Hosea 6.1-6

'Your love is ... like the dew that goes away early' (v.4)

Through these words of Hosea, God makes it clear that the people are complacent about God's forgiveness, mercy and love. Indeed, their love for God is like the morning dew – fleeting and short-lived – and the people seem to take no heed of God's judgement.

Holy Week brings us face to face with the all-embracing love of God revealed in Jesus Christ, which is as sure as the coming of the dawn each day, but that does not mean we should take God's mercy and forgiveness for granted. The empty tomb does not make light of the cruel cross.

If we are tempted to live the enormity of this day a little too complacently because we already know the truth of Christ's coming resurrection, may these verses urge us to sit with the grief and desolation. Holy Saturday is often filled with activity and preparation for Easter Sunday, but it is a day with its own unique character as we wait while Christ lies dead in the tomb.

Today is a day to sit with the emptiness and the absence. It is a day to rekindle our desire for God and for our love to grow deeper and more steadfast, so that when Easter Day dawns, the overwhelming reality of Christ's life and love being stronger even than death will be all the greater and our shouts of 'Alleluia' ever more joyful.

Grant, Lord,
that we who are baptized into the death
of your Son our Saviour Jesus Christ
may continually put to death our evil desires
and be buried with him;
and that through the grave and gate of death
we may pass to our joyful resurrection;
through his merits,
who died and was buried and rose again for us,
your Son Jesus Christ our Lord.

COLLECT

Reflection by **Rachel Treweek**

45

Monday 6 April

Monday of Easter Week

Psalms 111, 117, 146
Exodus 12.1-14
1 Corinthians 15.1-11

Exodus 12.1-14

'This day shall be a day of remembrance for you' (v.14)

Here we are presented with detailed instructions on how the Israelites are to prepare for their escape to freedom from slavery in Egypt. Yet, the wonderful blend of symbolism and practicality is not all about a one-off event. This is the institution of an annual act of remembrance to be kept throughout the generations. It reflects the identity of the people which is inextricable from their story and their relationship to God and who God is – the God of rescue in and above all. This rescue and freedom will be fulfilled in Jesus Christ who centuries later will be spoken of by John the Baptist as the Lamb of God (John 1.29) – the one who will sacrificially give up his life to free us from self-destruction.

Just as the institution of the Jewish Passover emphasizes the importance of yearly remembrance, so too we remember Christ's bloody death and self-giving love, not only in the days of Holy Week, but also in our regular sharing in the Eucharist.

Yet these verses also pose an uncomfortable challenge as to how the story we tell and the freedom we receive as we are fed by Christ, are to be faithfully passed on from one generation to another. Children and adults alike are to find their life and story caught up in the story and transforming love of God. What might that mean today for the way we live and share our story among the people and places of our lives?

COLLECT

Lord of all life and power,
who through the mighty resurrection of your Son
overcame the old order of sin and death
to make all things new in him:
grant that we, being dead to sin
and alive to you in Jesus Christ,
may reign with him in glory;
to whom with you and the Holy Spirit
be praise and honour, glory and might,
now and in all eternity.

Reflection by **Rachel Treweek**

Psalms 112, 147.1-12
Exodus 12.14-36
1 Corinthians 15.12-19

Tuesday 7 April
Tuesday of Easter Week

Exodus 12.14-36

'And bring a blessing on me too!' (v.32)

In today's reading, we continue to be immersed in the drama of the Israelite's Exodus from Egypt, with the emphasis being not only on preparation but also on remembrance in years to come.

In the relief of rescue, there is also terrifying tragedy. Just as all the Israelites are favoured, the Egyptians experience appalling suffering. It is not only Pharaoh and those directly responsible for the Israelite's misery who bear the consequences.

There are no glib explanations, but in every remembrance of Jesus Christ celebrating the Passover supper with his friends as the lamb about to be slaughtered, whether in Holy Week or in every act of Holy Communion, we recall that he broke the bread and pointed to his death for love of the *whole world* – for us, all people and all creation.

Pharaoh, in his arrogance and malevolence, speaks somewhat perversely of blessing in finally being rid of the Israelites, but there is conceivably a nudge for us in those words. In this week of resurrection hope, as we give thanks for God's forgiveness and blessing, how might we pray for those in our world who are viewed as dishonourable simply by association with those who lead them? And dare we go further by seeking blessing, reconciliation and restoration for the perpetrators who inflict misery on other people?

God of glory,
by the raising of your Son
you have broken the chains of death and hell:
fill your Church with faith and hope;
for a new day has dawned
and the way to life stands open
in our Saviour Jesus Christ.

COLLECT

*Reflection by **Rachel Treweek*** | 47

Wednesday 8 April

Wednesday of Easter Week

Psalms 113, 147.13-end
Exodus 12.37-end
1 Corinthians 15.20-28

Exodus 12.37-end

'The whole congregation of Israel shall celebrate it' (v.47)

As we continue reading instructions about the Passover, it is striking that everything relates to the *whole community* of the people of God. Even though each individual in the household shall eat the Passover meal (with some uncomfortable exceptions: foreigners and bound or hired servants), there is nothing individualistic about it. The identity of the individual is intertwined with the identity of the household and the community.

In our journey of faith as Christ's followers, much is said about personal prayer and growth in discipleship, but we are not always so good at emphasizing that this focus is inextricably linked to being God's people and members *together* of the body of Christ. Receiving the bread and wine in the Eucharist, when we celebrate Christ's fulfilment of the Passover, is deeply personal, but it is also a proclamation of our common baptism and our belonging together.

This truth may not be congenial when there are tensions and disagreements, whether within specific worshipping communities or across the wider Church, yet we are called to keep our eyes, ears and hearts open to recognizing what it means to be part of the whole people of God and to live as such. Without this, our identity in Christ is rendered meaningless.

COLLECT

Lord of all life and power,
who through the mighty resurrection of your Son
overcame the old order of sin and death
to make all things new in him:
grant that we, being dead to sin
and alive to you in Jesus Christ,
may reign with him in glory;
to whom with you and the Holy Spirit
be praise and honour, glory and might,
now and in all eternity.

Psalms 114, 148
Exodus 13.1-16
1 Corinthians 15.29-34

Thursday 9 April
Thursday of Easter Week

Exodus 13.1-16

'... the Lord brought you out from there by strength of hand' (v.3)

Today's reading contains the instructions for the first-born of all animals and humans to be consecrated to the Lord and the first-born sons to be redeemed. In this we recognize the themes and melodies that are to be played out in the future in the giving of God's only Son, fully human and fully divine. Also, we continue to listen to the repeated motifs of remembrance throughout the generations, and the focus on the community. We hear again the repeated refrain of the people going out and coming in as the Israelites are reminded of their departure from Egypt and as they look towards their entering into the promised land.

In both the going out and the coming in, there is an emphasis on the presence of God's hand and strength. This is echoed in the words 'The Lord will keep your going out and your coming in from this time on and for evermore' (Psalm 121.8), often used as a Christian act of blessing at pivotal points in the story of an individual or a community.

As we journey beyond Easter week and into all that the future holds, the strength and presence of God are unchanging. Let us not forget God's faithfulness in all we face as we look both back and forward.

God of glory,
by the raising of your Son
you have broken the chains of death and hell:
fill your Church with faith and hope;
for a new day has dawned
and the way to life stands open
in our Saviour Jesus Christ.

COLLECT

Reflection by **Rachel Treweek**   49

Friday 10 April
Friday of Easter Week

Psalms 115, 149
Exodus 13.17 – 14.14
1 Corinthians 15.35-50

Exodus 13.17 – 14.14

'... you have only to keep still' (14.14)

This passage is full of human wandering and wavering. The people of Israel's physical wandering in the desert is matched by an internal wavering in their relationship with God. As they question their journeying, there is distrust, dissatisfaction and fear. Yet in it all, God's leadership and authority are unwavering. This is visibly symbolized in the pillars of cloud and fire that are always in front of the people for their guidance.

But it is not only the Israelites who are wavering. The Egyptians, for very different reasons, also have a change of heart. Both peoples seem minded to take matters into their own hands as they allow themselves to be driven by pressing desires and fears. And then comes that clear exhortation from Moses to the Israelites to not be afraid and to stand firm.

In our own lives, individually and together, there is often much oscillation of heart and mind. It is when we are at our most fearful and uncertain that we strive to exert greater control and fail to acknowledge our dependence on God. As we look to move beyond this Easter week, what might it mean for us to stand still and trust that God is for us, even when the present and the future might look and feel uncertain?

COLLECT

Lord of all life and power,
who through the mighty resurrection of your Son
overcame the old order of sin and death
to make all things new in him:
grant that we, being dead to sin
and alive to you in Jesus Christ,
may reign with him in glory;
to whom with you and the Holy Spirit
be praise and honour, glory and might,
now and in all eternity.

Reflection by **Rachel Treweek**

Psalms 116, 150
Exodus 14.15-end
1 Corinthians 15.51-end

Saturday 11 April

Saturday of Easter Week

Exodus 14.15-end

'So the people ... believed in the Lord' (v.31)

As with so many of our Scripture readings this week, this is a cinematic passage that is easy to visualize. In the Israelites' great escape through the parting sea, there is much stopping and starting involving people, chariots and waters. Yet ever since the people of Israel left Egypt, there has also been a stopping and starting of belief and trust in God.

Through Moses' obedience and trust in the lifting and stretching out of his hand, the people of Israel view the stopping of the waters, followed by the awful drowning of the Egyptians. We then learn that because the Israelites had seen God's great work, they now believed in the Lord and in Moses. Yet, if the people had chosen to keep the eyes of their hearts and minds open from the very start and not rely only on their physical sight, they might have been able to see God's steadfast presence with them at every point in their story.

In our own lives, there can be a sense of stop–start in our relationship with God, particularly when our trust and belief is dependent on what we see and experience. Whatever life looks like on the surface, God's faithfulness and love are unchanging, and nothing can stop the arrival of God's kingdom.

God of glory,
by the raising of your Son
you have broken the chains of death and hell:
fill your Church with faith and hope;
for a new day has dawned
and the way to life stands open
in our Saviour Jesus Christ.

COLLECT

Reflection by **Rachel Treweek** | 51

Morning Prayer – a simple form

Preparation

O Lord, open our lips
and our mouth shall proclaim your praise.

A prayer of thanksgiving for Lent *(for Passiontide see p. 50)*

Blessed are you, Lord God of our salvation,
to you be glory and praise for ever.
In the darkness of our sin you have shone in our hearts
to give the light of the knowledge of the glory of God
in the face of Jesus Christ.
Open our eyes to acknowledge your presence,
that freed from the misery of sin and shame
we may grow into your likeness from glory to glory.
Blessed be God, Father, Son and Holy Spirit.
Blessed be God for ever.

Word of God

Psalmody *(the psalm or psalms listed for the day)*

**Glory to the Father and to the Son
and to the Holy Spirit;
as it was in the beginning is now:
and shall be for ever. Amen.**

Reading from Holy Scripture *(one or both of the passages set for the day)*

Reflection

The Benedictus (The Song of Zechariah) *(see opposite page)*

Prayers

Intercessions – a time of prayer for the day and its tasks, the world and its need, the church and her life.

The Collect for the Day

The Lord's Prayer *(see p. 51)*

Conclusion

A blessing or the Grace *(see p. 51)*, or a concluding response

Let us bless the Lord
Thanks be to God

Benedictus (The Song of Zechariah)

1   Blessed be the Lord the God of Israel, ◆
     who has come to his people and set them free.

2   He has raised up for us a mighty Saviour, ◆
     born of the house of his servant David.

3   Through his holy prophets God promised of old ◆
     to save us from our enemies,
         from the hands of all that hate us,

4   To show mercy to our ancestors, ◆
     and to remember his holy covenant.

5   This was the oath God swore to our father Abraham: ◆
     to set us free from the hands of our enemies,

6   Free to worship him without fear, ◆
     holy and righteous in his sight
         all the days of our life.

7   And you, child, shall be called the prophet of the Most High, ◆
     for you will go before the Lord to prepare his way,

8   To give his people knowledge of salvation ◆
     by the forgiveness of all their sins.

9   In the tender compassion of our God ◆
     the dawn from on high shall break upon us,

10 To shine on those who dwell in darkness
         and the shadow of death, ◆
     and to guide our feet into the way of peace.

Luke 1.68-79

**Glory to the Father and to the Son
and to the Holy Spirit;
as it was in the beginning is now:
and shall be for ever. Amen.**

Seasonal Prayers of Thanksgiving

Passiontide

Blessed are you, Lord God of our salvation,
to you be praise and glory for ever.
As a man of sorrows and acquainted with grief
your only Son was lifted up
that he might draw the whole world to himself.
May we walk this day in the way of the cross
and always be ready to share its weight,
declaring your love for all the world.
Blessed be God, Father, Son and Holy Spirit.
Blessed be God for ever.

Easter

Blessed are you, Lord God of our salvation,
to you be praise and glory for ever.
As once you ransomed your people from Egypt
and led them to freedom in the promised land,
so now you have delivered us from the dominion of darkness
and brought us into the kingdom of your risen Son.
May we, the first fruits of your new creation,
rejoice in this new day you have made,
and praise you for your mighty acts.
Blessed be God, Father, Son and Holy Spirit.
Blessed be God for ever.

At Any Time

Blessed are you, creator of all,
to you be praise and glory for ever.
As your dawn renews the face of the earth
bringing light and life to all creation,
may we rejoice in this day you have made;
as we wake refreshed from the depths of sleep,
open our eyes to behold your presence
and strengthen our hands to do your will,
that the world may rejoice and give you praise.
Blessed be God, Father, Son and Holy Spirit.
Blessed be God for ever.

after Lancelot Andrewes (1626)

54

The Lord's Prayer and The Grace

Our Father in heaven,
hallowed be your name,
your kingdom come,
your will be done,
on earth as in heaven.
Give us today our daily bread.
Forgive us our sins
as we forgive those who sin against us.
Lead us not into temptation
but deliver us from evil.
For the kingdom, the power,
and the glory are yours
now and for ever.
Amen.

(or)

Our Father, who art in heaven,
hallowed be thy name;
thy kingdom come;
thy will be done;
on earth as it is in heaven.
Give us this day our daily bread.
And forgive us our trespasses,
as we forgive those who trespass against us.
And lead us not into temptation;
but deliver us from evil.
For thine is the kingdom,
the power and the glory,
for ever and ever.
Amen.

The grace of our Lord Jesus Christ,
and the love of God,
and the fellowship of the Holy Spirit,
be with us all evermore.
Amen.

An Order for Night Prayer (Compline)

Preparation

The Lord almighty grant us a quiet night and a perfect end.
Amen.

Our help is in the name of the Lord
who made heaven and earth.

A period of silence for reflection on the past day may follow.

The following or other suitable words of penitence may be used

Most merciful God,
we confess to you,
before the whole company of heaven and one another,
that we have sinned in thought, word and deed
and in what we have failed to do.
Forgive us our sins,
heal us by your Spirit
and raise us to new life in Christ. Amen.

O God, make speed to save us.
O Lord, make haste to help us.

Glory to the Father and to the Son
and to the Holy Spirit;
as it was in the beginning is now
and shall be for ever. Amen.
Alleluia.

The following or another suitable hymn may be sung

Before the ending of the day,
Creator of the world, we pray
That you, with steadfast love, would keep
Your watch around us while we sleep.

From evil dreams defend our sight,
From fears and terrors of the night;
Tread underfoot our deadly foe
That we no sinful thought may know.

O Father, that we ask be done
Through Jesus Christ, your only Son;
And Holy Spirit, by whose breath
Our souls are raised to life from death.

The Word of God

One or more of Psalms 4, 91 or 134 may be used.

Psalm 134

1   Come, bless the Lord, all you servants of the Lord, ♦
    you that by night stand in the house of the Lord.

2   Lift up your hands towards the sanctuary ♦
    and bless the Lord.

3   The Lord who made heaven and earth ♦
    give you blessing out of Zion.

**Glory to the Father and to the Son
and to the Holy Spirit;
as it was in the beginning is now
and shall be for ever. Amen.**

Scripture Reading

*One of the following short lessons or another suitable
passage is read*

You, O Lord, are in the midst of us and we are called by your
name; leave us not, O Lord our God.

Jeremiah 14.9

(or)

Be sober, be vigilant, because your adversary the devil is
prowling round like a roaring lion, seeking for someone
to devour. Resist him, strong in the faith.

I Peter 5.8,9

(or)

The servants of the Lamb shall see the face of God, whose name
will be on their foreheads. There will be no more night: they will
not need the light of a lamp or the light of the sun, for God will
be their light, and they will reign for ever and ever.

Revelation 22.4,5

Into your hands, O Lord, I commend my spirit.
Into your hands, O Lord, I commend my spirit.
For you have redeemed me, Lord God of truth.
I commend my spirit.
Glory to the Father and to the Son
and to the Holy Spirit.
Into your hands, O Lord, I commend my spirit.

Or, in Easter

Into your hands, O Lord, I commend my spirit.
  Alleluia, alleluia.
Into your hands, O Lord, I commend my spirit.
  Alleluia, alleluia.
For you have redeemed me, Lord God of truth.
Alleluia, alleluia.
Glory to the Father and to the Son
and to the Holy Spirit.
Into your hands, O Lord, I commend my spirit.
  Alleluia, alleluia.

Keep me as the apple of your eye.
Hide me under the shadow of your wings.

Gospel Canticle

Nunc Dimittis (The Song of Simeon)

Save us, O Lord, while waking,
and guard us while sleeping,
that awake we may watch with Christ
and asleep may rest in peace.

1   Now, Lord, you let your servant go in peace:
    your word has been fulfilled.

2   My own eyes have seen the salvation
    which you have prepared in the sight of every people;

3   A light to reveal you to the nations
    and the glory of your people Israel.

Luke 2.29-32

**Glory to the Father and to the Son
and to the Holy Spirit;
as it was in the beginning is now
and shall be for ever. Amen.**

**Save us, O Lord, while waking,
and guard us while sleeping,
that awake we may watch with Christ
and asleep may rest in peace.**

Prayers

Intercessions and thanksgivings may be offered here.

The Collect

Visit this place, O Lord, we pray,
and drive far from it the snares of the enemy;
may your holy angels dwell with us and guard us in peace,
and may your blessing be always upon us;
through Jesus Christ our Lord.
Amen.

The Lord's Prayer (see p. 51) may be said.

The Conclusion

In peace we will lie down and sleep;
for you alone, Lord, make us dwell in safety.

Abide with us, Lord Jesus,
for the night is at hand and the day is now past.

As the night watch looks for the morning,
so do we look for you, O Christ.

[Come with the dawning of the day
and make yourself known in the breaking of the bread.]

The Lord bless us and watch over us;
the Lord make his face shine upon us and be gracious to us;
the Lord look kindly on us and give us peace.
Amen.

Love what you've read?

Why not consider using *Reflections for Daily Prayer* all year round? We also publish these meditations on Bible readings in an annual format, containing material for the entire Church year.

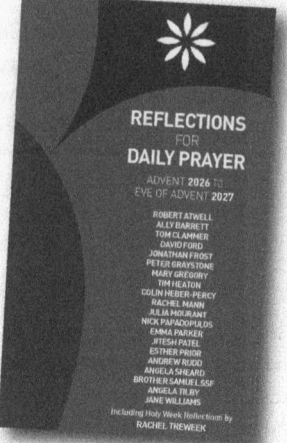

REFLECTIONS
FOR
DAILY PRAYER
ADVENT 2026 TO
EVE OF ADVENT 2027

ROBERT ATWELL
ALLY BARRETT
TOM CLAMMER
DAVID FORD
JONATHAN FROST
PETER GRAYSTONE
MARY GREGORY
TIM HEATON
COLIN HEBER-PERCY
RACHEL MANN
JULIA MOURANT
NICK PAPADOPULOS
EMMA PARKER
JITESH PATEL
ESTHER PRIOR
ANDREW RUDD
ANGELA SHEARD
BROTHER SAMUEL SSF
ANGELA TILBY
JANE WILLIAMS

Including Holy Week Reflections by
RACHEL TREWEEK

The volume for 2026/27 will be published in May 2027 and features contributions from a host of distinguished writers including:
Robert Atwell, Ally Barrett, Tom Clammer, David Ford, Jonathan Frost, Peter Graystone, Mary Gregory, Tim Heaton, Colin Heber-Percy, Rachel Mann, Julia Mourant, Nick Papadopulos, Emma Parker, Jitesh Patel, Esther Prior, Andrew Rudd, Angela Sheard, Brother Samuel SSF, Angela Tilby, Jane Williams.

The reflections for Holy Week 2027 are written by **Isabelle Hamley.**

**Reflections for Daily Prayer:
Advent 2026 to the eve of Advent 2027**

ISBN 978 1 78140 524 6
334 pages • Available May 2026

Can't wait for next year?

You can still pick up this year's edition of *Reflections*, direct from us (at **www.chpublishing.co.uk**) or from your local Christian bookshop.

**Reflections for Daily Prayer:
Advent 2025 to the eve of Advent 2026**

ISBN 978 1 78140 496 6
334 pages • Available now